SHADYBROOK HOUSE
P. O. Box 98
Mentor, Ohio 44060

journal for life

discovering faith
and values through
journal keeping

Part Two:
Theology from Experience

George F. Simons

ACTA
Foundation for Adult Catechetical Teaching Aids
Chicago, Illinois

To the friends new and old whose theology I have experienced.

With gratitude to Betty and Mari
   who make sure that I get my work done
      by doing a great deal of it,
         and to the Danforth Foundation
           whose generosity provided me
              with time and space to renew my acquaintance
           with earth and heaven.

Copyright © 1977 Life in Christ,
division of ACTA FOUNDATION
Library of Congress Catalogue No. 75-17161
ISBN No. 0-914070-10-X
Printed and manufactured in the
United States of America

Contents

Page 1 — **1** RELIGION AND EXPERIENCE

Page 9 — **2** PEELING LABELS

Page 15 — **3** COMPONENTS OF RELIGION

Page 24 — **4** THEOLOGY FROM EXPERIENCE

Page 33 — **5** BE THE SCRIPTURES

Page 40 — **6** BANNERS I CARRY

Page 47 — **7** LIVING IN A RELIGIOUS SOCIETY

Page 56 — **8** BREAKTHROUGHS

Introduction

> **Religion Can't Slow Production, Tribunal Rules**
>
> Nottingham, England
>
> A Pakistani Moslem who held up a factory's production line while he prayed five times a day on his knees, was justly dismissed from his job, an industrial tribunal decided yesterday.
>
> The tribunal was told that Abdul Rashid felt obliged by his religion to stop work at set times and pray for up to half an hour.
>
> Rashid had appealed against his dismissal by Metallifacture, a light engineering company, which employed him on its production line.
>
> The tribunal was told that his colleagues, who agreed he was a good worker when not praying, had been worried about losing their bonuses because the production line was held up while Rashid prayed.
>
> Rashid is now working as a priest in a mosque.
>
> *Reuters* *

I need a fix!
    Anonymous, 20th Century

    Impatience seems to be our national disease (dis-ease?). While younger people have been described as a "switched-on generation," almost all of us have come to rely on solid state circuitry in one way or another. Solid state means instant sound, instant picture, instant response, no warm-up, no waiting. When this circuitry fails, we are perhaps most annoyed with the human factors, the inept assembler, the slowness of the repairman, the delay in getting replacement parts. We demand that it be fixed.

* *San Francisco Chronicle,* 28 April 1976
Permission granted: Reuters

Introduction

This need for the instant "fix" transfers itself to how we look at our own human organism. It's not only the "junkie" who needs a fix. We pop pills, demand the impossible of our physicians, dentists and psychotherapists. We behave this way in the area of personal development, too. I want to "fix" myself, get rid of faults and acquire virtues, go on crash diets to lose or gain weight, quit smoking, get in shape. By sheer force of will sometimes some of these things are accomplished. More commonly we tell the tale of momentary success followed by crushing defeat. Failure is then celebrated by a round of self-denunciation, setting us up, after a more or less long wallowing in despair, for new attempts to fix ourselves. There is an alternative to this "fix-flop" sequence of behavior. We can let go of this mechanistic, solid state view of humanity and exchange it for a more humane and realistic image of ourselves as living organisms. Certainly, we are beings who can be both wounded and diminished. But also, with time and care we have within us the capacity to heal and grow.

Rather than a series of instant fixes, we as persons need to set up for ourselves a dynamic of living, a pattern of existence which is basically sound, satisfying, and non-injurious. It begins with and continually includes listening to our inner selves, to the needs of the life within us, not allowing them to be drowned out by the clamoring pressures of the speed society in which we find ourselves daily. Slowing down, observing, savoring are antidotes for this common malaise. Often overweight people are told that they eat too much because they eat too fast. They are advised to slow down, take more and smaller bites, chew and, above all *taste*. In this, the richest of all nations, consumption of all kinds goes on at a frantic rate, cars, homes, furnishings, appliances, clothes, and sex partners grow obsolete long before we've come to get acquainted with them and appreciate them. Is it any wonder that our very bodies tell us about spiritual and moral indigestion and flabbiness that is going on? The chase is suicidal.

Journal keeping is one way of savoring, digesting, healing and growing. It is a way of monitoring ourselves, discovering our own preferences and needs, a way of teaching us about ourselves, an antidote to overdosing. The pause that truly refreshes cannot be bought in a bottle. You must learn to take it from yourself — for yourself. Keeping a journal will help you do this.

The first of this series of workbooks in journal keeping is called *Foundations*. The techniques it contains are meant to be the basis for an ongoing program of personal growth by providing some fundamental procedures and directions. As such, it provides information about the process of keeping a personal journal and exercises to facilitate the beginnings of this practice. It also contains exercises which help those who are learning journal keeping together to become acquainted with each other and work well as a group. It yields an

Introduction

initial look at the religious self, the level of self-esteem, perspectives on how the individual sees and relates to God and religion with its institutions and traditions. There are many suggestions for further explorations of less explicitly religious issues. This second workbook, *Theology from Experience,* is a natural continuation of this search for faith and values through journal keeping. While it can be used independently of the *Foundations* book by individuals or groups, there is much valuable information there about journal keeping and group discussion which is not repeated here.

WHY THEOLOGY FROM EXPERIENCE?

Our religious systems have often reflected rather than resisted the contemporary world's "instant fix" mentality. "Cheap grace" has been made available through quickie confessions and come-to-the-altar professions of faith. It's like winning the lottery and having money in the bank to free us from ever having to work again. Here, perhaps we can learn from some of the very rich. Money in the bank can result in aimless decadence or insatiability, or, it can lead the well endowed person to the realization that money isn't everything. Now that he or she has it, there still remains the task of creating a meaningful life of work, relationships and play, a task sometimes more hindered than helped by affluence. Few of us enjoy the security of the financially sure, but we do need to learn how to find meaning and enjoyment in who we are, what we do and in the people around us. Our priorities, our values, our religious beliefs and practices will either help us do this or need to be replaced with ones that do. We need a theology based on experience, tested by experience, enriched by experience. This volume of *Journal for Life* is aimed at the development of such a theology or philosophy of life.

It is subtitled *Theology from Experience* because it proposes some simple ways for individuals and groups to use personal experience for religious and ethical growth. By applying these methods you can be led to a deeper appreciation of the richness of your own life and the wisdom that it contains. You will find that religion flows out of your spirit as much as into it. As you work, you will discover that old concepts and beliefs take on new meanings, stagnant areas are revitalized and attitudes are reformed. This process can be a source of energy for both personal and institutional renewal.

In *Theology from Experience* you will be doing theology first hand, engaged in the primary task of each human being, making sense out of your life. Yet these are only exercises, ways of going about our personal work. They are not the goal of religious practice but a process, an asceticism of sorts. They are tools you may use to clear the rubble from the doorway of the temple. Use them as you need them. Don't get stuck with them. Don't stand on the

Introduction

threshold when it's possible to enter the sanctuary. Answer when your name is called.

> *Every person is entitled to engage in a project, through which he comes to terms with life's essentials for him, on which he can put his stakes, through which he may fulfill himself by taking hold of reality as reality appears and applies to him.*
>
> Paul Pruyser

Journal keeping takes time. So does everything else. Taking time out for ourselves, real time out to pay attention to our inner needs and fantasies is perhaps the hardest single thing for most contemporary Americans to do. Our culture has thrust upon us two devouring needs, productivity and belonging. The first writes into my very nervous system the rule that everything I do must be useful, productive, profitable. Even my recreation and my play (I work hard at both!) are looked upon simply as restoratives for my working capacities. The second need urges me to endless efforts to belong, to fit in, to be one of the gang. Between these two birds of prey the possibility of a personal spiritual life is picked to death. Journal keeping gives you one more challenge to be alone and non-productive, or, to speak in traditional terms, to enjoy solitude and contemplation.

Writing itself is a private act, and the kinesthetic activity, the bodily engagement, involved in the use of pen and paper helps us to focus and concentrate. Children and older people are often condemned as dreamers and do-nothings when their natural freedom from adult "responsibility" leads them to flights of fantasy and times of "inactivity." This repression of the spiritual life makes the children into drones who ultimately retire into senility rather than sagacity. We need alternatives to this disastrous cultural track.

> *Wasting time is one of the privileges of being human.*
>
> Joel

If journal keeping, or any other regular spiritual exercise, is to work for you, it will take time. For most people, especially for those who need it most, it will be painful and wrenching to begin to take this time alone and stay with it. Once journal keeping begins to work for you, it will usually sustain itself, demanding your time simply because it contributes richly to your life. Even so, contemplative solitude is always somewhat in danger because of the inexorable contrary demands of the environment. Even those who enter monasteries carry the world in their bloodstream, capable of avoiding contemplative life by being "busy about many things." An early monastic founder once complained how men who in the world had argued over high finance, as monks, became contentious over erasers in the monastery writing room.

Introduction

As an introduction to solitude and contemplation the process of journal keeping presented in these books has two particular advantages. It is a specific concrete activity which engages our minds, emotions and physical activity in the act of writing. For me personally this means that I slow my mind down to the speed at which body and mind can cooperate in writing. Stemming my mania in this way, I strip fewer gears. Secondly, beginning the process of journal keeping in a group, in addition to the growth possibilities which lie in the group process itself, uses the dynamics of belonging and the commitment to work to free us from social pressures and workaholism. Making a contract to work regularly with others engages us in regular private reflection. Experiencing the benefit of this reflection will keep us moving individually when the group work has come to an end. Journal keeping is time wasted, and wasting time is something we desperately need to do. It is time taken out of our personal and corporate plunge to disaster, time to see what we are doing to both our personal psycho-bio-system and to the political and material ecology of the world about us, time to redirect. If we can't start to do it on our own, perhaps it will come about with collusion and collaboration — by conspiracy. Moreover, to each of us belongs the responsibility so succinctly summarized by the New Zealand poet James Baxter, to "tell other ignorant people what you in your ignorance think you know."

> *It's so much nicer to have a whole room full of teachers rather than just one.*
>
> *Amy*

The arrangement of materials in this book includes separate directions for individuals working alone in a personal journal as well as for groups of people who keep journals privately but find it valuable to gather regularly to experience working together and sharing their explorations. There's much to be said about both the risks and rewards of sharing. What is most important, however, is that you are totally in control of your own choice to share or not share. This book is constructed to allow both options and provide guidance for both individuals and groups. In the Appendix you will find some discussion guidelines. They build upon those contained in the first volume of *Journal for Life*. Persons working in groups for the first time will find that the gradual introduction of these guidelines will be enormously helpful as aids to better communication.

This is a workbook. It will not self-destruct. It is up to you to destroy it. Write in it. Draw in it. Cut out the parts that mean something to you. It is not just for reading but for doing, too.

> *I don't believe in God — I think that's clear to you people — but I do believe in a lot of the things believers believe in.*
>
> *J.*

Introduction

This process of personal spiritual growth through journal keeping is not meant for religionists of any specific denomination or faith. The exercises in this book are useful for "believers" and "non-believers" alike. They have been used successfully by persons coming from both Western and Eastern religious traditions, Protestants, Roman Catholics, Jews, Hindus, both by those who are deeply involved in their religious life as by those who are uncertain or agnostic. If you are working as a group, you may choose to work with co-religionists, to explore your variety and diversity within a common framework. On the other hand, you may choose to enrich this experience by including in your group persons of various religious and philosophical persuasions. Individuals coming from other personal standpoints and values systems help each other to encounter their different traditions and experiences with freshness — they provoke new insights for each other. Habits of reflection, contemplation and shared growth are non-denominational. We can share them with each other. It is a matter of fact, however, that content and illustrations in this workbook are largely drawn from Judaeo-Christian sources. We have adhered to this working bias as being realistic for most of the people who have worked and do work with this program. Many of those alienated from these matrices of faith have been touched by them and continue to be faced by at least their traces in our cultural inheritance.

Needless to say the processes and procedures contained in *Journal for Life* are intended for persons of normal stability. Anyone who feels regularly overwhelmed by what takes place in the course of these exercises or by other critical events affecting emotional balance, should most certainly seek professional guidance.

Ladies and Gents

I have made a very deliberate effort throughout these pages to avoid the use of sexist language. I am not simply kowtowing to the women's movement or to threats of harassment from female friends and co-workers, but acknowledging as fact that the identity implications of much of our language prejudice consciousness and personal growth if they are not checked from the outset. What sexist usages remain here come either in the form of quotation — I felt it would be a nuisance to both of us to lace the lifted passages again and again with "[sic]" — or in linguistic prejudices for which there seem to be no practicable solutions at present, or from the deep waters of my subconscious where "lady" and "nigger" and other assorted trash resulting from my living as a white male American all these years have settled. To this last, I can only protest that I am making efforts to improve this submarine ecology.

1
Religion and Experience

Every dogma, creed, and theological concept is based on an original experience, and if corporate religious life does not focus on experience, (the warm, live, 'feeling-ful,' vibrant presence of each individual and the meaning of his uniquely immediate existence), corporate religious life will be sterile, even at its very best.
James Lynwood Walker

REVELATION AND EXPERIENCE

Those religionists who quail about experience as if it were the enemy of all that is established or revealed in religion must bear in mind that what are called revelations occurred *in the experiences* of people. When revelations and traditions are presented to others by word, text, symbol or ritual, they become new experiences to be encountered in their own right in the present. Be sure that what has been revealed will be revealed again only as it coheres with and emerges from the experience of new generations. When experience is minimized, discouraged, revelation shrivels; when experience is accepted, encouraged, the seed of revelation will germinate, sink deep roots, and the flowers and the fruit it contains will come into being.

It is perhaps good that we learn the stories of revelation, the myths of our race when we are young. They become an endowment, a *vademecum* for life. But comprehension, the inner "aha," comes only with experience. The fruit falls when it is ripe. I encountered *Faust* as literature when I was in my teens. I only began to experience its truth and the temptation it tells of when I was a middle-aged college teacher. Buried in books, I momentarily raised my head and caught a glimpse of what looked like life passing me by. It was a moment in which I knew it was possible to sell my soul for youthful years and springtime love. The short entry in my journal was written with tears and tells all:

> "I am listening to Gounod's *Faust* now and hearing it for the first time. *Ce que voudrait Dr. Faust c'était 'la jeunesse'* [what Faust wanted was youthfulness.] [he sings]
> '*A moi tes désirs* [Let me have its passions]
> *A moi ton ivresse* [Let me have its intoxication]
> *A moi . . .*' [Let me have . . .]
> Then Barbara (a beautiful young woman) stopped by to visit."

So it is with our scriptures, our myths, and our truer than life fiction. It is important to teach these things, to point them out on the tree as fruit that *will* become edible. To pluck and eat when the moment is ripe carries its own learning in the event and the aftermath, but to force our children to eat prematurely is to fill their stomachs with bitterness and to taint their perception with fear or disgust. As a result, they will hesitate or refuse to approach that fruit again and fail to be nourished by it in season. Hungers go unsatisfied, heart and mind malnourished.

We can miss out on experience in other ways. Events, encounters and feelings can be dismissed, overlooked, depreciated, lost. We may move so quickly from one minute to the next that we enjoy no moments whatever. "Minute" and "moment" are often interchanged in common speech — yet what a difference. The first is a measure of time saying nothing about quality; the second is a part of *moment*ous, a sip of the eternal. Movement without awareness. Rushing. Consumption without taste. Performance without purpose. Self-consciousness without consciousness. Minutes without moment.

Experience is the fabric of religion. The Judaeo-Christian scriptures are themselves a collection of such experiences — human experience. History is the vehicle chosen by Jews and Christians to reveal the divine presence. Theology is a tool for comprehending, analyzing, preserving and handing on this experience. Liturgy and ascetic practices are settings and events in which these experiences are actualized, and made available.

The exercises in religious awareness which this book contains facilitate a return to experience. Remember. Feel. Experiment. Let happenings tell their own story. Let experience fill out "that which has been handed down."

THEOLOGY AND EXPERIENCE

Theology, as a tool of religion, may be a reasoning from things seen to things unseen. Whether or not this is so, it must always begin with things seen, that is, with experience. But religion is then, before it can become grist for rational extrapolation, a feeling, a perceiving and a naming, an assertion about experience itself. It is rooted in the intuition, the knowing which takes place before speculation. Moreover, the theoretical answers of theology and philosophy become less satisfying, less useful and less certain as they travel from the person who is the center of religious feelings and beliefs to deductions and predictions. Experience is the beginning and end of the journey of religious faith. Things taken "on faith" are middle places, bivouacs on the road. Faith in the Judeao-Christian tradition begins by *hearing* and ends by *seeing*.

Theology can be learned in two ways. We can digest others' descriptions of their religious experience as we do when we read theologians and spiritual writers, or when we listen to or use prayers composed by others. Most people, at least at first, learned what they consciously know as theology or religion in this way. This level of learning theology has advantages and drawbacks. Insofar as our individual experience resonates with that which we are told, read or listen to, we become truly engaged in the religious experience. Yet, social pressures of conformity to group beliefs, the subtle sway of rhetoric, the wanting to believe, obey and belong may take us years away from our own experiences to a place where our beliefs and feelings and our needs are consciously or unconsciously at war. A divided self results, possibly lacking energy, commitment, a person unable to see and feel, a person who does inappropriate things and feels confused or guilty about them. This almost inevitably happens to some degree in the passage from childhood to adulthood.

Then usually in our thirties we begin theology in another way. It may be a long, uneasy and circuitous route to the certainties which are so easily proposed by the first way, but it is indeed our doing theology rather than learning of it. Its method begins with an acceptance of experience as the norm of belief, its chief interpreter. What I do, what happens to me, the feelings, the needs which surround my deeds, events, encounters, accidents — these are the teachers of what the universe is all about. They will unlock for me the history, the myths, the poetry and the fiction of my race.

Once I have encountered my own experience, I am on my own ground. Sometimes the encounter itself is all that I need. At other times it is important for symbols and stories of my own experience to connect with those of others. A proverb, a piece of wisdom, a verse or event of scripture becomes my own in a unique way. Thus the uncommonness of each person enters the communion of belief. With experience mature belief can begin. We begin to believe and trust each other out of the *experience* of truthfulness and caring.

Much religious education has proceeded to tell us what God is like, or grace is like, for example. There is always a *yes* and a *no* in every affirmation. While this may have some validity in a metaphysical framework — nothing ever *is* what it *is like* — psychologically such procedure is like the experience of *yes-but*. When someone says, "Yes, I'd like to come but I don't have the time today," the real message, the fact follows the *but*. It is what is heard and acted on. Thus the attempt of theology or philosophy to defend the transcendent to distinguish it from the commonplace has frequently served to make it inaccessible. Experience, rather than being a clear channel, is silted up with qualifications. Teaching exercises, worship experiences and experiements frequently suffer the same fate. We are told what to expect or experience. Commentary rules rather than the rites or experiences themselves.

Every religious metaphor, experiment, rite, needs to be a self-validating experience, understood as whole and true in itself even though it is limited, i.e., not the whole truth of something. There are more and varied experiences of the same person, thing, event, which if realized will give us more and more knowing in the fullest sense of the word.

THE PRIMACY OF EXPERIENCE

When we speak of the theology of experience, we do not mean simply the analyzing of experiences so that they yield up their meaning and thus confirm or deny older theological assumptions or teachings. Our task is not to verify the past but to find truth for our present. The past may help. It can act as a servant and a teacher.

Yet, "experience *is* the best teacher," that is, when we are allowing ourselves to *have* experiences, not just explore them intellectually. The event itself is already the teacher, not by explaining the past or creating a new past which the future will look to for explanation, though it may do both these things. When one has entered an experience and passed through its cycle, then it is possible and may be valuable to speak of the meaning of the experience, to profess its meaning for the individual.

Experience can be tyrannical, too. Deep personal experiences or beliefs based on them tend in conversation to be projected into absolutes, into statements about how the world is rather than simply how it is for me. So do not be too quick to project the meaning of the experience into an absolute, suggesting that it is bad or good or true or false for others, or all people or even for myself in all times and situations. It is important to avoid assigning a premature meaning to experience. Meanings which seem like interpretations, which seem to come more from the head than the guts, should be held suspect, suspended. Living through the experience actively and perceptively is far more important for inner meaning than its enunciation and interpretation.

In this respect, it is interesting to note that for early Christian society (to say nothing of anthropological evidence for most non-Western cultures) *experience* of rites and rituals, for example of initiation, was primary. Explanation, catechesis about the rite, if it took place at all, was secondary and followed rather than preceded an event. Contemporary Roman Catholic liturgical practice for one has tended to precede, accompany and follow the rites with commentary. This is hardly the climate for helping individuals and congregations to openly encounter the event and experience its symbols. Rather, it seems directed toward prejudicing the experience so that if it is encountered at all, it can be encountered only in one predetermined way. The need for such commentary seems to spring up from a deeply felt insecurity about the power of rites and symbols themselves or about the perceptive capacities of the congregants rather than from a sureness of their efficacy.

Here as in many other places in our culture, people are told what to feel and how to feel rather than presented with an experience or context in which they are helped, encouraged, allowed to feel as fully as possible. Frustration results and further alienation follows.

BELIEF AND EXPERIENCE

> *It seems likely that far more people in our time experience neither the presence of God, nor the presence of his absence, but the absence of his presence.*
>
> R. D. Laing

It has become popular to look at belief as something belonging to the ancients or to primitives or to children. The ancients knew no debate about the existence of God or other spiritual agencies. In a time when the lives of men and women are seen as politically expedient by our CIA and military machine, when an aborted fetus is euphemistically described as "the tissue," we may be almost humored by the naivete of primitives who make a great to-do placating the spirits of the animals they hunted for food and who even ate their enemies with *reverence*. For me, as a child, religion, God, Spirits were as real as anything else in the realm of my experience — I can remember quick turn-around glances, attempts to catch my guardian angel unawares in some visible state. (The angel was always too quick for me.) There were, of course, atheists among the ancients, just as there are dishonest shamans among primitives, and as any department store Santa knows, there are precocious rationalists among the three year olds. Yet, the exceptions only highlight the fact that there is something about certain ages, cultures and times of life that make them more conducive to belief than others. What is it? Let's begin to go after this question by asking what things in our own culture and behavior are inimical to belief.

> *Education implants a logical lens in the skull. Whoever looks through that lens can see nothing sacred. The Mass is an event in comparative religion. A Maori tangi* [funeral ceremony] *is an event in comparative anthropology. Sex is a physical union of parts of the body. Death is a statistical occasion.*
>
> James K. Baxter

Certain peoples are reported to have an abhorrence for giving their true names to others. Mothers in some cultures never call their children by their right name, lest an evil spirit overhear and harm the child. Superstition? Not if one realizes the power in naming. "Sticks and stones may break my bones but names will never hurt me" was a chant I learned as a child to defend myself from the hurt I actually felt when others called me names. It was a lie.

The greatest part of what we call education today takes place through naming, that is, through language, words. And the language that is usually chosen is that of the detached observer, the so called "objective" language of the scientist, whether the scientist be a physicist or a theologian. We look for reasonable, factual data, evidence that can be replicated by experiment. And when we have so dissected a poem or a frog or an angel or God, using tools which by definition exclude feeling, mysticism and organic wholeness, should we be surprised that the specimen has died? What a paradox that scientific examination whose purpose is *to know* makes agnostics, *unknowers* out of so many, that the search for the physical *norms* of nature leaves the searchers in a state of anomie, *normlessness!* With these shallow empirical abstractions we go about a subtle campaign of demythologizing (a theologian coined that term), devalorizing people's lives. We explain away whatever means something to people (or to ourselves) then wonder why "nothing means anything any more." What kind of Christology is it that produces words, words, words and no living Word?

Education is both a short cut and a short circuit. Educated about the danger of thin ice, I may be saved from drowning. Other experiences of water and fragile footholds will keep me from skating too close to the sign which shouts, "Danger, Thin Ice." Classroom education about winds and currents and the operation of a sailboat may certainly be of use to me, but I may well capsize and drown if I believe that any amount of head work will give me the skilled hands and the agility I need to work the mainsheet and tiller where the weather meets the sea. When it comes to skills, real education and experience are inextricably entwined.

Our attitudes are shifting. The boat is being rocked precariously. Erving and Mariam Polster sum up the scene so well:

> *Not too long ago, little attention was paid to immediate experience under the assumption that personal involvement while learning disrupted the objectivity essential for clear-headed conceptualization. Learning* requires *a sense of personal immediacy, however, as well as theoretical perspective; like one hand washing the other, they are inseparably linked . . .*
>
> *Now, with the exciting proliferation of new behaviors and values, people are caught in mid-air. They are fascinated by the fresh liveliness possible in first-hand experience, but they lack the integrative cohesion which theory provided by giving meaning and perspective to the things they needed to do and feel. Theory and knowledge remain suspect, not because of inherent worthlessness, but because of their historic isolation from action. Without theoretical orientation, however, action is vulnerable to oversimplified and glib imitativeness — even mimicry — and to the use of the gimmick.* *

Rationalism has often assaulted and sometimes co-opted religion. It has at times methodically gone about attacking beliefs. At other times it has used religion without believing in it, assuming that religion is functional — it keeps people moral, honest, satisfied, etc.

Note that it is rationalism as a closed system that I am objecting to, not rationality. Increased powers of rationality in later adolescent and post-adolescent years are important for maturation. Part of this maturation is the

---

* Erving Polster and Miriam Polster, *Gestalt Therapy Integrated* (New York: Brunner/Mazel, 1973), pp. 2-3.

destruction of useless religious structures. We do need a common sense, pragmatic rational regulation of religion in our personal and community lives, but this is quite the opposite of a rationalism in which no tolerance is left for inner experience. Theory is important, but it remains alive only in reciprocity with what we do and feel. Knowledge with feeling is best; facts to which we attach values directly are those which we learn most easily, retain most readily and attach ourselves to as truth on a theoretical and practical level.

Education as such need not be the enemy of belief but emphasis on analysis without parallel efforts at synthesis with experience have often made it not only a source of disbelief but helped it to erode its own foundations. "Words are cheap" runs the old saw. But worse than unkept promises is language without respect, dealing with people and things and experiences in words as if reality were not greater than the words. People used to fear the magician, the witch and the warlock, ones who could speak a formula and cast a spell. Now TV commercials and diplomatic language do it more effectively. The same temptation exists in education and via education has made its way into our common culture. Jargon replaces spells in a world seeing itself as mechanistic.

The irony of it all comes full swing when the well educated must go to great expense to reacquire the vitality of peasant styles and natural foods, when worn Levi's cost more than new ones.

However we have been becoming more and more aware of the fact that values and world view are acquired by observation, imitation and absorption of what others do, as much as or more than what they say. How else could members of families and religious communities in some instances experience a supportive community of love and in others a reign of terror all seemingly generated by the same ideology, the Gospel of Love? It is the subtleness of emphasis in actual practice which gains the day in experience and in the formation of the individual's religious outlook.

James William McClendon astutely observed that:

> *The best way to understand Theology is to see it, not as the study about God (for there are godless theologies as well as godly ones), but as the investigation of the convictions of a convictional community, discovering its convictions, interpreting them, criticizing them in the light of all we can know, and creatively transforming them into better ones if possible.* *

To do this we must go even a step further, starting our investigation with the awareness, experiences and convictions of the individuals who make up this strange assortment of communities we call society. What better starting place than ourselves and perhaps a study group becoming friends? Let's begin.

* James W. McClendon, *Biography as Theology,* (Nashville: Abington Press, 1974), p. 35.

2
Peeling Labels

It is said that when you give a child the name of a bird, it loses the bird. It never sees the bird again but only a sparrow, a thrush, a swan, and there's a good deal of truth in this. We all know people for whom all nature and art consists of concepts, whose life, therefore is entirely bound up with objects known only under labels and never seen in their own quality.

Joyce Cary

We have a name for just about everything in our experience, a label which, like the labels on cans and bottles and boxes, tells us about the shape, size and uses of what is inside the container. More and more we come to rely on truth in packaging. Today, it's possible for me to open the cupboard, look at the label on a can, pull it down, run it through the electric can opener and dump it in the stew with hardly a look at its insides. Packaging and labeling is not only a convenience, it has become a necessity in our technological society where often infinitesimal refinements make it virtually impossible for even the trained eye to distinguish one transistor from another, one serum or pill from another.

But much labeling, putting names on things, has a price, and the price is a diminishing of the quality of our contact with reality. Maybe this is nowhere as evident as in the stereotypical names we give to other human beings. "Nigger," "honky," and "spic" are ways of robbing others of their humanity and allowing ourselves to do other nasty and sometimes lethal things to them. But even the most non-malicious, everyday names of things, feelings and events have this same quality of keeping us once removed from the experience of that which is named.

Occasionally it helps us to get beyond our judgments and our labeling, to peel off the label and really examine the contents, to get beyond the normative names which we place on things, to feel, taste, smell, hear and see afresh and to be descriptive of what we sense and what the sensing is like in us. Inevitably, we return to names — that's the unique part of our human abilities for knowing and communicating. But, if we've peeled some labels and examined the contents, we may come up with more accurate labels, and even the old ones which we paste back on will signal realities better, be richer in meaning for us as a result of our contact with what's beneath them.

Peeling Labels

Working Alone with your Journal

1.) Begin with a familiar object or two. Peel the label, that is, forget about the name and use every sense to explore the object as fully as possible. Write in your journal or use this page to record as descriptively as possible what you feel, taste, smell, hear and see.

12 JOURNAL FOR LIFE

2.) Go back on an event of the day. Allow it to replay itself in your mind. Again describe fully what happened in your journal or on this page. Be careful to be descriptive rather than making inferences and judgments. For example, instead of, "A sinister man sat next to me in the bus today," write, "The man who sat next to me in the bus today was unshaven and shabbily dressed. He smelt of alcohol. His left hand twitched nervously. I felt afraid of him." Write the description below or in your journal.

3.) Peel the label from a religious experience or concept (a teaching or precept). Describe what lies beneath it for you personally, not only what you have been taught, but what has taken place for you in this experience or around this concept. Again be as specific and concrete about what happened and how you feel about it. Use this page or your journal to do this.

Working in a Group

Use the three steps given in the instructions for working alone. Writing will help you focus awareness. However you may, instead of writing, take turns describing objects and/or persons in the room, events which happened during the day or are happening now within the group. Help each other to be concrete and specific, to avoid judgments and inferences. Proceed to the religious experiences and concepts in the same way. In each instance listen carefully to whomever is speaking. Our insights and perceptions can be sharpened as we share in the vision and experience of others. If your group is large, you may choose to work in threes and fours. If you do so, save some time at the end for each person who wants to share with the whole group how he or she feels about the session.

This approach can be used over and over again. Individually we can avoid prejudices and snap judgments by looking beyond labels. We can also slow down, savor life and need to consume less as we enjoy more. As groups making plans and decisions, we can learn to look more carefully and respect each others' needs and feelings by pausing to peel away attitudes and judgments which are holdovers from other situations and past perceptions.

Notes for Group Leaders

If journal keeping is a new experience for your group, your first meeting might be one to discuss individuals' feelings about it and to introduce some of the Guidelines for Discussion. The materials found in Chapters 2 and 3 of the first volume of *Journal for Life* and the Guidelines found in the Appendix will be helpful.

Choose a comfortable place to meet, one that will be free from interruptions and will allow all the members to sit in a circle to see and speak to each other, as well as to divide into smaller groups or pairs for some exercises.

No specific materials are required for this exercise, unless the group wishes to write before discussing. Then pens and journals or copies of this workbook are necessary.

3
Components of Religion

The roots of religion are so numerous, the weight of their influence in individual lives so varied, and the forms of rational interpretation so endless, that uniformity of product is impossible.
                                               Gordon Allport

16 JOURNAL FOR LIFE

What we want and don't want right now in our lives may be related to good or bad experiences. It may also be related to things others told us to fear or expect or to look for and enjoy. How we go about explicit religious living, how we shape and participate in the rites, norms and activities of religious traditions is also related to our experiences, personal and shared. Now we are going to look at our encounters with religion and see what they have to tell us about our preferences and ourselves.

A little fantasy might help to get our minds and pencils moving, so . . . use your imagination to conjure up a situation such as that on the next page.

Components of Religion 17

You have decided to establish a new religion/philosophy of life or reform a traditional one. Below is a list of some of the usual components of religion. Evaluate each according to how desirable you would find it in your new faith or philosophy. Some examples of what these might mean are given. Do not be limited by them—they are only suggestions. If for example "mystical experiences" mean something quite different than highs, feelings of oneness with God, nature, etc., trust your own definition. *Desirable* mean *you want them* for some reason or other. Consult yourself.

COMPONENTS OF RELIGION	Very Desirable	Somewhat Desirable	Uncertain	Somewhat Undesirable	Very Undesirable
1. *Mystical experiences* highs, feelings of oneness with God, nature					
2. *Congregation/fellowship* others working with you in a religious context, doing religious things together					
3. *Rituals* fixed ways of worship, fixed forms or words, or structures, or ways of going about certain religious activities					
4. *Explicit Moral Injunctions* definite do's and don't's coming from an authority or tradition					
5. *Feast Days, Holy Days* definite times, days, seasons set aside to commemorate an event/idea important to those who celebrate it; celebration of of life cycle events, birth, death, marriage, sickness					
6. *Mythology* stories told to explain why the world is as it is, why we are/act as we are/do; stories which tell why/how we can grow, change, be saved					
7. *Familial Religious Practices* religious things done together, at home; prayers at various times, bible reading, festive meals					

COMPONENTS OF RELIGION	Very Desirable	Somewhat Desirable	Uncertain	Somewhat Undesirable	Very Undesirable
8. *Scriptures* basic traditional religious documents of continuing authority, e.g., Torah, New Testament, Vedas					
9. *God(s)* divine being(s)					
10. *Meditation* means of reflecting on religious data, self, experiences					
11. *Savior Figure* a person who mediates between the present and the fulfilled human condition, e.g., Jesus, Buddha					
12. *Invoking the Divine, Prayer* an ability to talk to the divine or ultimate reality or to intercessory or saviour figures					
13. *Sexual Taboos* special restrictions around sexual activity					
14. *Dietary Laws* imposed or chosen fasting, e.g., Kosher, vegetarianism, abstinence					
15. *Purgatory/Reincarnation* ways of evolving/improving the human condition beyond death					
16. *Ministerial Persons/Priesthood* priests, ministers, rabbis, elders, deacons					
17. *Proselytization* efforts at making converts, missions					
18. *Doctrine on Death/Immortality* a definite belief about what happens at death, about the existence/non-existence of the individual after death					
19. *Separation of Church and State* a more or less distinctly legislated separation of the religious and governmental institutions and their claims on the public					

COMPONENTS OF RELIGION	Very Desirable	Somewhat Desirable	Uncertain	Somewhat Undesirable	Very Undesirable
20. *Deals with Suffering/Evil* the religion tells us something about the purpose or meaning of these					
21. *Social Action/Criticism/Prophecy* religious institutions or persons speak out for or against public policies, culture, evaluate events					
22. *Charismatic Gifts* speaking in tongues, foretelling the future, healings					
23. *Coherence with Scientific Theory* religious belief is not opposed to what we know about the world, humanity, from other researches					
24. *Sages, Gurus, Spiritual Directors* people who can help/teach about the spiritual quest					
25. *Art, Aesthetics, Symbolism* graphic representations, images of religious things					
26. *Monasticism* closed community of men and/or women whose purpose is to love and live/grow religiously					
27. *Standards of Admission/Membership* personal qualities or acts or beliefs required before a person is admitted to a religious group					
28. *Hymns or Songs or Chants*					
29. *Asceticism, Self-Discipline* techniques or methods for spiritual growth					
30. *Holy Places, Shrines, Pilgrimage* places to travel to or be at which have particular religious power or significance					

COMPONENTS OF RELIGION

	Very Desirable	Somewhat Desirable	Uncertain	Somewhat Undesirable	Very Undesirable
31. *Contemplative Life Style* — hermitages, retreats, ways of getting with one's self					
32. *Celibacy* — renunciation of sexual activity/attitudes for religious reasons					
33. *Confession* — admission of failures, guilt, sin to another or others					
34. *Physical Touching* — kissing, embracing, imposing hands					
35. *Ethnic Solidarity* — religious belief related to common parentage, national or racial origin					
36. *Organized Charities* — efforts of religious groups/institutions to serve the poor, sick, imprisoned or people with other sorts of disadvantages					
37. *Occult Lore* — secret or esoteric doctrines of special significance known only to specially initiated or advanced members within a religious group					
38. *Concern with Nature* — nature seen as having special spiritual significance					
39. *Bingo, Bake Sales* — non-religious fund raising efforts for religious groups					
40. *Work Ethic* — salvation seen as related to how hard/well one works					
41. *Preaching/Sermons*					
42. *Cosmology* — a special religious understanding of how the world came about or is constituted					

COMPONENTS OF RELIGION	Very Desirable	Somewhat Desirable	Uncertain	Somewhat Undesirable	Very Undesirable
43. *Emotional Outpouring* a definite place for expressions of joy, anger, sorrow, etc., in religious gatherings					
44. *Public Demonstrations* processions, parades, protests, etc.					
45. *Orgy* times of all out expression/satiation of emotions, desires, instincts, e.g., dance, inebriation, sexual acts, etc.					
46. *Drugs* altered states of consciousness deliberately induced by chemical means					
47. *Saints* persons successful in their religious quests who, beyond death in a new state of being can be of help to those still on their spiritual journey					
48. *Other* . . .					
49. *Other* . . .					
50. *Other* . . .					

When you have completed these pages, you have a large reservoir for continued journal work. Look at your preferences. Did any of your answers surprise you? Which ones elicited the strongest evaluations? Which were uncertain? Any of these would be a good starting point for further reflection. Take one and begin. Write about your personal history with this religious component. What happened to you with it? What have others told you about it? What have you come to believe about it? What emotions does it arouse? If there are unresolved feelings, you might engage it in a written dialogue. Talk to the event and let it talk back to you. Discuss or argue with it. Do this to your own satisfaction with as many of the components as you feel a need to. Perhaps in the process other components not listed in the questionnaire have come to mind. You may choose to work with them in similar ways.

In a Group

If you are working in a group, you may want to complete this questionnaire before you meet — that will provide more time for discussion. You may also do the questionnaire when you meet. If you finish before others, please try not to disturb them.

You may want to form smaller groups to discuss your decisions. Try to observe these guidelines in your discussion.

Present your feelings as clearly as you can. Wherever possible discuss the personal experiences that are at the root of your decisions, e.g., "I am opposed to asceticism because when I tried fasting last Good Friday, I . . ."

Do not argue about another's experiences, e.g., "You shouldn't feel that way because . . ." Do not piggyback, e.g., "That reminds me of the time I . . ." Our purpose here is to learn as much as we can about the uniqueness of our own and each other person's experiences and values.

Proceed in any order that you wish; ask for further information when you need it, but make sure each group member gets equal air time.

If you do your discussion in threes or fours, regroup toward the end of your time together so that each person who wants to can give a summary of his or her experience.

Follow up this meeting with as much personal journal work as you find useful in exploring the components of religion.

Components of Religion 23

Follow Up Work

Whether you do this exercise privately or in a group, it is not meant to be just a hypothetical look at the components of religion. Some consequences suggest themselves.

> *What things can I do to make desirable components a part of my religious life?*
>
> *How can I affect my religious institution in this direction or away from undesirable components?*
>
> *Or, even before I do either of these things, I might look at opportunities to experience certain components afresh.*
>
> *What do others' experiences with these things suggest for new approaches on my part?*

Notes for Group Leaders

Each person should have a copy of *Journal for Life* (Part Two) with the above "Components" questionnaire and a pen.

This questionnaire is capable of generating endless amounts of discussion. Group members may want to meet on it more than once. Subsequent exercises in this program will provide other means for exploring some of the issues raised by this components questionnaire, so it will be better to move on after one or two meetings, knowing that you can return to it at another time if this seems useful.

4
Theology from Experience

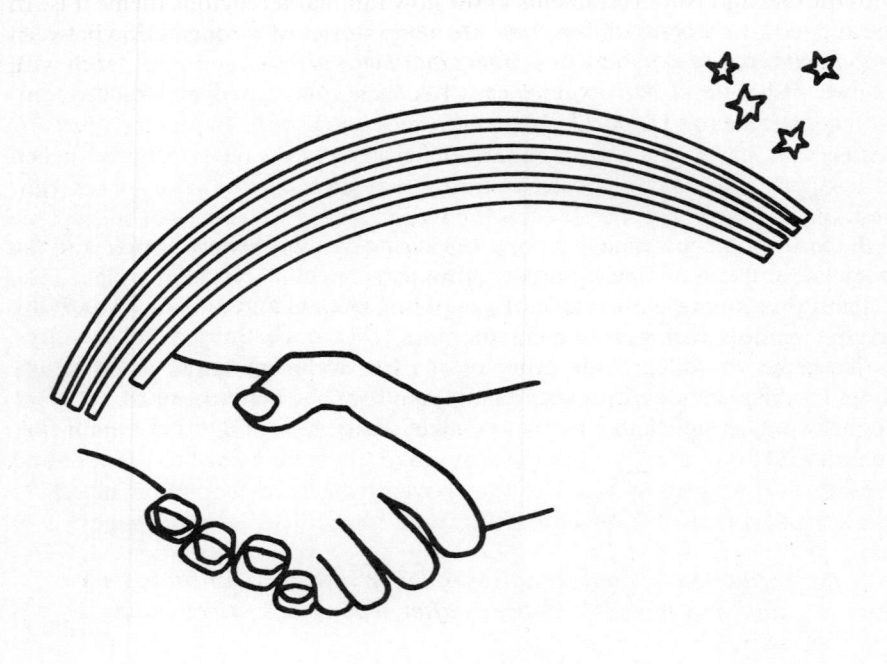

Choices between one ontology and another are not made on purely intellectual grounds but have much to do with the basic feeling for life and the emotional appreciation of the self and the world that each person acquires from his personal experiences.

Paul Pruyser

Religion and philosophy, either outright or because they exist in the values and practices of communities we belong to, hand on to us from our earliest years a collection of assumptions about life, concepts to be believed and a variety of moral and ethical demands to be observed. Life alone teaches us their meaning; only experience interprets them for us. In the work of this chapter we will explicitly use our personal experiences as a resouce for exploring how we understand religious and theological concepts.

Take an idea like *reconciliation* for example. Those of us who are familiar with the Old and New Testaments know how familiar a religious theme it is. In the Judaeo-Christian tradition there are many stories of reconciliation between individuals like Jacob and Esau, Pilate and Herod, Peter and Paul, each with its own wisdom and instruction for us. Reconciliation also occurs on the community and cosmic level. God becomes reconciled with humanity after the Deluge and leaves a rainbow to mark the event. God is repeatedly reconciled with Israel in the course of their stormy marriage. At the core of the New Testament is the belief that Jesus is the reconciler *par excellence* of this people with God. The gospel preaches forgiveness of offenses between people and the forgiveness of sins as signs that this ultimate reconciliation is taking place. The Vatican chose reconciliation as an issue to be explored and celebrated as many ways as possible during the last Jubilee Year.

Yet "reconciliation" like so many of the theological words of Latin and Greek derivation, remains formidable and distant. Sermons and religious writings are often chains of words like "reconciliation," "community," "charity," "initiation" and the like. It makes them very hard to listen to and to read. For instance, if I look at the above list of words and allow myself to speak the first thing that comes in to my mind, I get the following images:

> *Reconciliation* — representatives of labor and management in dark suits and ties shaking hands after signing a contract ending a strike.
> *Community* — a pleasant hamlet nestled on a green hillside, houses and outlying farms, a church spire and a main street.
> *Charity* — The American Catholic Bishops' annual Thanksgiving clothing drive.
> *Initiation* — college freshmen streaking across campus wearing their dinks (only).

Say the words to yourself and jot down here or in your journal the images that you get as immediate reactions to hearing them. Don't pause for reflection, just record whatever association comes no matter how holy or outrageous it may be.

These are part of the baggage that each of us carries into our listening and understanding, and if we were to expand and reflect on them in our journals or in our minds we could find ourselves making judgments about their rightness or usefulness for our religion or philosophy of life. I am going to ask you to suspend that judgment and do something else.

THEOLOGIZING FROM EXPERIENCE

Take "reconciliation" as an example. Using all that I know about it, I try to distill its essential ingredient or characteristic. I "peel the label." I attempt to come up with an everyday word that gets at the heart of it for me. When I do this, I come up with "forgiveness." For the sake of learning this process, I'm going to ask you to work with "forgiveness," too. Later on, I will give you some suggestions about how other words may be broken down and explored. Once you've done it a few times, it will be easy to proceed on your own.

Theology from Experience 27

Have your pen and journal ready and put yourself in a comfortable place where you can both reflect and write.

> *Close your eyes and concentrate on forgiveness for a while, on your personal experiences with forgiveness.*
> *Let the experiences run freely through your mind.*
> *When you feel ready, choose an event of forgiveness that stands out in your mind, the last time you forgave someone or some other significant act of forgiveness on your part.*
> *Who was it?*
> *What happened, what was the offense that had to be forgiven?*
> *What happened that made forgiveness possible?*
> *What took place in the act of forgiveness?*
> *How did you feel before forgiving?*
> *During?*
> *After?*

Tell the story in your jounal or on the blank page below. When you have finished, stop, reread it, and allow it to sink in. Stay with it long enough to feel its impact. Leave it only when you are satisfied.

Then, when you are ready:

> *Choose another story, about the last time or an important time that you sought forgiveness from someone else.*
> *For the moment, keep it an event between individual human beings — you can apply what you learn here to your relationships to communities or to God at a later point.*
> *Whose forgiveness did you ask?*
> *Picture that person.*
> *What had you done?*
> *How did forgiveness take place?*
> *What did you do?*
> *What did you say?*
> *How did you feel beforehand?*
> *During?*
> *After?*

Again when the memory is vivid, write the account in your journal or in the space provided below. Reread it and reflect on it as you did for the first story.

MY EXPERIENCE OF FORGIVING

MY EXPERIENCE OF BEING FORGIVEN

As a result of this experience, a number of learnings will suggest themselves to you. Treat them as learnings which emerged from these particular situations. They may be suggestions about other reconciliations that need to take place in your life. If suggestions come, make note of them, but rather than fashioning absolute ideas, hard and fast rules about the nature of reconciliation, stay with experience. If there is a burning need for a reconciliation to take place in your life, something that calls for forgiving or being forgiven or both, do what you feel is necessary to get started in this direction. If it is impossible for you to make real contact with the person you want to be reconciled with either because that person is not accessible to you (unknown location, dead, etc.) or you cannot bring yourself to make the contact, you're not ready yet — begin by having the reconciliation take place in fantasy, and if it suits you, by fashioning prayer around it. The questions used above when you dealt with reconciliation the first time might be useful for stimulating your fantasy and making it flow. Imagine the event from the beginning, what is said and done. By fantasizing in this way and recording the fantasy in your journal and re-reading the fantasy both after you've finished it and once again, later — perhaps after a week — you may be able to touch for yourself the attitudes, the fears of disaster, whatever obstacles stand in the way of reconciliation. You may be able to deal with these so that forgiveness is possible. You may decide that it is not yet possible. Either way, you will know much more about it and about yourself and be a step closer to what needs to happen for you in respect to reconciliation.

APPROACHES TO OTHER RELIGIOUS CONCEPTS

I am going to give you a short list of some approaches to traditional religious concepts which I have used. Do not expect a single reflection to tell everything about the religious concept. If it tells something about your experience with it and enriches your understanding and impels you to work with it, you will be doing theology. You will no doubt be able to think of other theological or philosophical concepts and everyday ingredients that you want to explore, even your own approaches to some of the suggested topics. Remember, nothing is too down to earth to provide grist for your theological mill. For most of us, the more everyday, earthy, pedestrian we can be in our reflections and fantasies, the more we will enrich our faith and our values system. Try these:

Providence — caring for someone; being cared for.
Initiation, Baptism — being brought into a family, community;
   bringing someone into your family, community.

Ministry — serving, being served.
Charity — loving; being loved.
Church — being alone; belonging together with others.
Spiritual Direction, Guruship — advising; being advised.
Sin — being hurt; doing hurt to another.
Liturgy — throwing a party for someone; being guest of honor.
Prayer — talking, listening.
Gospel — getting good news; giving good news.
God — being a father/mother; having a father/mother.

By now I'm sure you see the structure for theologizing from experience. Let me summarize. Select a concept from your tradition or simply an idea you would like to explore further. Identify one of its everyday ingredients. Explore both the active and passive poles of that ingredient, i.e., reflect and write about it both as it is done to you, as you experience it, and, as you do it to others, as you experience being the one who acts or gives. At least at the beginning use questions like the ones we applied to forgiveness to make your account specific, and alive. *What took place? With whom? When? Where? What led up to it? What did you feel? During? After?* Use recent or outstanding experiences — they will be more vivid.

Theologizing as a group

This is a process that a whole group of people can do together. Sit in a comfortable circle and have the leader or one of the group members begin by instructing the participants to close their eyes and relax. A few deep breaths will help. Then, very slowly, with significant pauses between each sentence have the leader read the questions on the reconciliation experience printed in italics on page 27, or a similar set of questions which you have prepared beforehand to explore the topic of your choice. When the group has had time to reflect, whoever feels ready and willing can share all or part of the experiences they reflected on. If the individual wants, discuss his or her experience with the group, share feelings, observations, questions which come to mind.

Before you do this session, it will be helpful to familiarize yourselves with the guidelines for profitable discussion found in the Appendix to this book. Obviously not everyone can or will want to share thinking and feeling in this way. But, we do inevitably learn, theologize, not only by talking about ourselves but from listening and becoming involved in others' stories, discussing our reactions, asking questions and from just letting them sink in. Sometimes it's hard to close a session like this. So many possibilities are raised and we feel the loose ends of our own and others' experiences. It will be helpful if you have a definite way of ending that will take care of these unfinished things by at least recognizing them. One way of doing this is to set aside the final twenty or thirty minutes (depending on the size of your group), and use it as a time when each individual has a minute or two to state succinctly what he or she is most aware of, feeling, unfinished with, whatever is most focal, and to do this without any comment or question from either the leader or any other members of the group.

Packaging Your Learnings

Don't expect to wrap up your reflection in a neat little package that contains all the answers for yourself or as a gift for someone else. Experience is not that tidy — neither is theology though lots of writers and preachers and teachers would have us believe it is so. In the long run the best teachers are those who help us go through a process to make our own discoveries, not those who simply plop the answers in our laps. Emergencies may call for quick, neat answers based on what we know and believe at a given moment. So, too, we live our everyday lives wholeheartedly deciding and acting out of who we are and what we know and the best information we can get. It must do, even though we are conscious of the possibility of mistakes and failures. But maturation in faith and personal growth is tied to ongoing experience and reflection. The ultimate book of theological wisdom is the book of your life. Theology books and scriptures show us some themes to compose upon; experience tests and actualizes them. Your journal is a way of staying in touch with *your* biography as it is being written. It provides ideas and alternatives for the chapter you are writing now and will affect the outcome of the story. A Jewish tale concludes with the line, "God created people because he loves stories." Learn to love your story, too. Care for it.

Notes for Group Leaders

Careful presentation of the theme in this exercise is a most important part of your task. If you are using a topic other than *reconciliation,* prepare the questions for the initial reflection thoughtfully and well in advance of the group meeting. When the time comes to present them, read them slowly and with significant pauses between each. It is not at all too much to allow up to five minutes for people to reflect on each side of a given issue.

5
Be the Scriptures

Jesus said, "Show me the coin used for the tax." When he handed them a small Roman coin, he asked them, "Whose head is this, and whose inscription?" "Caesar's," they replied. At that he said to them, "Then give to Caesar what is Caesar's, but give to God what is God's."

Matt. 22:19-21

I am a twenty-five cent piece, a bicentennial coin. One side of me is very proud of the two hundred year history of my nation. I feel proud in this heritage, marching on into the future with a sense of destiny, rich in the resources and accomplishments of the land that my parents chose to settle in, never taking it for granted. The other side of me is more the quarter of every- day business. I am reminded that I am used for all kinds of transactions. "In God we trust" is written on me in very small letters — too small to be read when I am buying something or finding my way into a vending machine. I am used to buy weapons as well as medicine, extortion as well as liberty.

Joe

I am only a little dime, just like a million other little dimes. A little worn, not too shiny. I wonder if anyone will ever notice me, care about me, or will I just be carried along like all the other junk in people's purses, spent without a second thought. Will there ever be some special purpose for me?

Marie

WHAT ARE SCRIPTURES?

Scriptures are records of religious experiences. They tell of the encounters of individuals and peoples with gods and spirits and the inner workings of their own persons. Sometimes they recount these meetings with histories and stories and parables; at other times they enjoin the wisdom, morality or poetry which flow from their dialogue with the transcendent. These sacred writings become the myths a people lives by, ways of seeing the world.

PROBLEMS OF SCRIPTURE STUDY

The world view with which most moderns live, however, is no longer consistent with the Bible or the Vedas or any other ancient mythology. The stories of creation and the designs of the structure of the universe which scriptures tell are not, if taken literally, consonant with the actual knowledge of these things told by physics, astronomy, geology and anthropology. For some people the choice seems black and white, either become a fundamentalist believer or an agnostic. Others use science and scholarship like a skillful scalpel which can be inserted in the biblical text to separate tissue from fat, that is, to isolate what is thought to be the kernel of truth from the cultural and historical limitations of its expression. This is a valuable endeavor. It pleases our sense of logic and our need for scientific consistency. But there are drawbacks. First, many of the fine scholarly distinctions are comprehensible only to the professionals who made them in the first place, or to other highly educated and skilled persons. Lay persons feel left with scriptures which are for them an uncertain trumpet, they are hesitant to accept or act on their own best interpretation. This keeps a number of people from reading the scriptures at all; others read them painfully with copious commentary alongside, hoping for the understanding which will enrich both faith and living. Disappointment frequently follows because of a second drawback. Exegetical surgery tends to leave the scriptures colorless, lifeless, incapable of speaking. The patient expires on the operating table. The insights of the exegete may be taken as a substitute for the scripture itself.

MAKING THE SCRIPTURES LIVE

Fortunately, side by side with scholarship there have been living applications of scriptures in the preaching and teaching and lives of sages and saints. Artists and poets and composers have frequently retranslated the scriptures into media which speak to our hearts and feelings as well as to our logic and reason. Archaic figures and remote events become credible when they are made into the matter of direct experience. They march out of the text, and our spirits are in step with them.

When this human engagement with the scriptures takes place, we understand the use of the exegetical arts. They are meant to guard the treasure, not to steal it. They hold keys to open it and prevent it from contamination. Our purpose in using the scriptures is not just to find ways of reading them which are not inconsistent with our contemporary scientific world view. On the contrary, they must be the fertile field in which individuals and communities can plant their own experiences of the transcendent and profound dimensions of everyday events and encounters as well as the import of history as it happens.

Many arts are needed to cultivate this harvest, but at the root of them all lies each individual's willingness to plant the seeds to become personally engaged with the text. It is a willingness to be and feel *in one's own way,* with one's own history, reactions and emotions, the inner core of those events whose profundity led others in generations long past to record them as sacred for us. One such method of personal engagement is suggested here — *be the scriptures.* Let's approach it in more detail.

Become the Story

One of the ways of finding truth in a story is to be that story, to try it on, act it out, to become in our fantasy and play the characters, events and props of the life drama it holds. Here we shall enter the theology which comes from experience in a new way as we allow the scriptural story to become the telling place of our story. We learn not only about the ancient story but about our own experience, and the relationship between the two comes to life.

This is a process which has as many applications as there are scriptural texts. It is very simple. Read a scriptural story or event. Then choose one of the characters, objects or metaphors and identify yourself with it. Allow your inner self to speak as if it were that person or object. Record in your journal what that part of you has to say. Look at the example at the head of this chapter. Reading the gospel story about the coin of tribute, two persons, Joe and Marie imagined themselves as coins which could be used for tax payments. Each of their meditations is unique. Joe's is centered around his consciousness as a citizen and the responsible use of buying power. Marie's is more personal, a more primary exploration of her own worth and purposes. Both are working with the inner person who will have to make decisions regarding God and Caesar. Sometimes these reflective identifications are as brief and incisive as Joe's and Marie's. On other occasions, "being the scripture" may involve an extended soliloquy of many pages.

Working in a Group

When working in a group with this technique, it is possible for each of the participants to choose a person, thing or happening in the story to journalize about and then to bring the whole story together by sharing from what each has written. For more dynamism and spontaneity, group members may cooperate to role-play the parts they have chosen. Individuals in the group could take turns casting and directing the others in the scriptural excerpts of their choosing. The object of this is not to reproduce the drama with precision but to allow the actors to freely bring themselves to their parts to continue and extend the dialogue to wherever it leads them. Use your journal to record learnings from this group activity.

In choosing the parts you will play do not be too judgmental. There is as much learning, sometimes more, in playing the "bad guys" or "ignoble parts." In our mental processes and frequently in religious preaching, much is lost because we choose only the parts we would like to see ourselves identified with and see others in the rest. So if you are using the Bible, don't miss out on being the serpent, the pharaoh and the Pharisee.

Notes for Group Leaders

Virtually any scriptural episode can be explored with the use of this technique. For group work spontaneity is important. Therefore, choose the scriptural passage just before you are about to set to work "being it." Some good starting places are:

> Old Testament moments of call and conversion, e.g.,
> Abraham, Moses, Jeremiah, David.
> The New Testament Parables.

You may do several of these in a group meeting, depending on how long the actual living out of the passage takes the participants. Remember, however, to leave ample time towards the end of the session for the participants to reflect together on the experience.

More Applications

Besides using this approach for private journal reflection or for group learning, there are other valuable applications. Lay people may use it to prepare for worship or to digest scripture used in worship or to plan the construction or embellishment of liturgies. Clergy can find it helpful as a technique for preparing talks and sermons. Teachers may use it as a classroom technique, artists and writers as a means of making the text graphic and colorful.

It is also a way of finding the truth in scriptures and stories of other religious traditions, classic mythologies and literature. Writings that one explores in this fashion are very hard to forget.

As you read the scriptures, look at them as models for work that you might want to do. Place yourself in the classical texts with your own thoughts and feelings. For example, after the pattern of *Job,* you might want to create a dialogue entitled, "My Argument with God," or as Job also argued with his friends, "My Arguments with my Friends about God and Myself." It is important for us to be truly ourselves with God in faith and in the process of sharing religion and values with others if our actual religious needs are going to be met. Fantasy arguments may help us to clarify what religious expectations have been laid upon us and what we ourselves have experienced and want.

Here in brief are some other scriptural excursions you might want to take in your journal writing and perhaps in your group sharing.

> *Jesus and the Samaritan Woman (Jn 4:7-30): Jesus tells the woman about her five husbands.*
>> *Make a list of five things that would be surprising or disturbing if you discovered that others knew about them.*
>>
>> *Or, make for yourself a list of things that you fear would convince others, if they knew about them, that you are a phony, or not the person you claim to be.*
>
> *The Worthy Wife (Prov. 31): The writer describes the qualities of an ideal wife in Old Testament times.*
>> *Make a list of the things which you would look for in another or do see in yourself which would make for being a good wife or husband.*
>>
>> *If you are married or in a relationship leading in the direction of marriage, you might compare these lists as well as lists of the qualities which you appreciate in each other.*
>
> *Talents (Matt. 25): Investing and burying talents.*
>> *Make a list of things you do well or feel you have potential for.*
>>
>> *Which are easy to talk about and to do?*
>>
>> *Which tend to get buried by fear of failure, embarrassment, etc.?*

6

Banners I Carry

Convictions may be distinguished from principles, in that the latter are the product of reflective thinking, have often a rather academic flavor, and are perhaps more often weapons for attacking others than guides for ourselves . . . while convictions are very often particular and immediate in form, and may not be consciously formulated by their holders at all, yet when we do find our convictions, we find the best clue to ourselves.

James Wm. McClendon, Jr.

Banners, placards, T-shirts and bumper stickers profess the sentiments and tout the causes of millions of Americans. While much of the display may be superficial and faddish, certainly a great amount of it is deadly serious. Broadcasting one's preferences and displaying one's commitments in the right place at the right time takes guts. Occasionally it's accompanied by the spilling of both blood and tears. Inevitably the sight of others showing their colors in public, demonstrating their loyalties and protesting injustices raises questions for me. Where do my sympathies lie? What do I stand for? When I ask myself these questions, the inquiry goes below the particular cause to a whole set of values and habits within myself. I support a particular presidential candidate because he or she seems to embody programs and values close to my own. By looking at the succession of causes we have espoused we can get another look at our faith or values system, its development, coinsistency and directions. This exercise is intended to help you do this.

Begin by making in your journal or on page 42 a list of the various causes — humanitarian, social, political, personal, religious, etc., — for which you personally have taken a stand, banners which you have carried in the past and ones which you still wave. Don't forget *yourself* as a possible one of these; perhaps you ran for club treasurer or city councilperson at one time. We are concerned here not just with the private sentiments you have or have had about certain things, but with issues on which you expressed yourself publicly to others and sought to enlist their support or involvement.

When you have completed your list, read it over. You might want to rearrange the issues in chronological order to note any pattern or progression. Select from your list one cause that you have abandoned and one cause that you presently espouse. (It will be even more interesting if these causes reflect a progression or change in opinion about the same subject.) Print each cause or a slogan which embodies it on the top of a separate page of your journal or use pages 43-44 for this purpose. Beneath, describe the cause as you see it and the story of your involvement with it. When you have finished this, answer these questions for yourself. Make your answers full enough to be satisfying to you. Don't be afraid to go off on tangents which seem important to you.

> *What do you find that your present cause and the one you have abandoned have in common? How do they differ?*
>
> *What has changed in you that is reflected in your new choice?*
>
> *What persons, places, circumstances ana events have had a part to play in the transition away from the old cause? In the undertaking of the new one?*
>
> *Does the idea of having a cause make you feel uncomfortable or full of energy or how? Describe the feeling — right down to the physical sensations if you can. What do these feelings tell you?*

MY LIST OF CAUSES

A PAST CAUSE

A PRESENT CAUSE

As a Group Activity

If you are working with others, after you have selected one abandoned and one present cause from your list, proceed in this manner. Print each cause or its slogan in bold letters at the top of a 5" x 8" card with a felt tip pen or crayon. Underneath the cause or slogan, write a sentence or two telling the importance of the cause for you, and how you became engaged in it.

With a piece of masking tape fix the present cause to your chest and ask someone nearby to put the abandoned cause on your back. Stand up and walk around silently in the group long enough for everyone to read everyone else's signs. Then silently choose a partner whose causes interest you and find a quiet corner to discuss them. This may be done in threes or fours if the size of the group and the available time recommend it. Allow each individual to explain his or her causes and history with them. Use the questions given above as a basis for continuing the discussion. You might also ask each other what it feels like to have other people looking at your back, i.e., your past.

Conclude by gathering the group together and allowing each individual to sum up in a sentence or two without rebuttal or comment what he or she felt and learned during this session.

Notes for Group Leaders

Have cards, markers and tape at hand. Make sure that the markers are bold enough to be seen by others at a reasonable distance. Remind the participants of the discussion starters found on page 41.

Changes in Personal Agenda

With this chapter we have entered into a new dimension of our exploration of theology from experience, that of ethics or morals. Religion and values are concerned not only with what we think and experience; they are clearly about what convictions we form, courses of action we decide upon and carry out. By a strange reciprocity, what I do tells me who I am, and how I see myself tells me what I am to do. Learning to know myself will also tell me what kinds of thoughts and activities refresh and renew me when I feel trapped, lost or confused. Looking at changes in your personal agenda as you have done in this exercise has several advantages. It gives you some concrete instances of change and growth. If you do it from time to time, it is a way of avoiding stagnation, of keeping your concerns from growing old and out of touch with reality.

The process you have experienced in this chapter can be expanded to include more than just the "banners" you have carried, the explicitly touted causes. For example, you can take a look at your past and pick out areas in which you have had a significant change of opinion or change of agenda in your life, a change of political party, a change in churches or beliefs, a decision to move to a new city or neighborhood. Perhaps you were once excited about retail sales and later decided to go into social work. Maybe you were once very liberal about changes in your church and now have decided to become much more conservative. If you fasten on these issues, these turning points and new courses, you will find in each of them a string leading into the inner world of your basic values and religious beliefs. Write about these changes of agenda in your journal, trying to become conscious of what takes place in you as you explore the road you came by, the junction and the new path chosen.

> *What influences were at work in you then?*
> *Where are these influences now?*
> *What groups or individuals, events or circumstances contributed most to your deciding to change?*
> *Were there some things lost in the change?*
> *How do you feel about them?*

As you work, there may be other important questions which suggest themselves to you.

7
Living in a Religious Society

Men speak of "doing their own thing" in our day. This may have a shallow meaning, a slogan for a pseudo-redemption through the liberation of every impulse. It may also point to something more profound, man's determination to be true to himself and his values in life.

Eugene Kennedy

In this chapter we want to spend some time getting a good look at the forces, particularly religious ones, which surround our decision making in everyday life. The exercise is based on the premise that if we know the kinds of influences that are working on us, we are freer to respond to them, to go along with them or to choose other alternatives for ourselves.

Each of us lives in a variety of social groupings. Some of these are very formal, legal and public. Being a citizen of the United States, of the State of Ohio, of the municipality of Vermilion, I exercise rights and bear responsibilities in each, I vote and pay taxes to each. Each provides me with services which I would otherwise not be easily able to procure for myself. I could move elsewhere in the world, but most other places would find me in relatively similar social groupings. I am born into a family, later choose perhaps to join with another to create a new family of our own. Here is a very direct and personal kind of society with its intimate give and take, its immediate advantages and costs.

Between the vast governmental societies and the close social groupings of the family, there exists an infinite variety of public and private groups to which I may belong. Some are very freely chosen; I seem to fall into others almost by necessity. There are churches, political parties, grade schools, high schools and colleges, unions and professional organizations, neighborhoods and communes, clubs and service organizations, sororities and fraternities, ethnic cadres and sporting teams, the variety is infinite. What seems true for each one of them, as far as the individual is concerned, is that each of them costs something and claims to give something. There are membership dues in the form of responsibilities if not dollars too, and benefits which accrue to the members; there is a price and a payoff. In certain situations the society may claim the price even though the indiviudal who pays it may not enjoy the payoff. One may be asked to die for one's country.

Most of the time, however, within our fulfillment of social responsibilities, we like to think that we keep individual freedom as a high priority. While this is not necessarily true of all societies, it seems right to many of us, even if practice at times belies the theory. Therefore we measure the quality of our living in society by assessing the relationship of the price to the payoff. Is the financial advantage of sharing a flat with a roommate proportionate to putting up with her noisy habits? Can we work it out to our mutual advantage?

This may sound very individualistic unless we remember that every payoff is not simply a matter of exclusively personal benefits. We work for general benefits and claim "broader causes" and "higher purposes." Whatever the personal satisfaction of "doing one's duty" or "following one's call," the participation of many individuals in certain societies is directed to objectives far beyond the participant. The zealous missionary, the social reformer, the

Living in a Religious Society 49

political campaigner, the presidential bodyguard, whatever their psychological satisfactions, may spend their energies and their lives as part of the cost of belonging to the order, the party or the White House Staff. Thus the payoff may be a conglomeration or a combination of various benefits both within and beyond the individual.

So too, there are penalties in society. The heretic is excommunicated, the gangster deported. The miscreant child may be sent to bed without supper, the burglar to prison. Even in the societies which we enter voluntarily, we play by the rules or pay the penalties, or leave the society, or possibly work to change the rules. Not all options seem open to us at all times.

Finally, since most of us find ourselves belonging to a number of societies simultaneously, we experience their conflicting claims upon us. The bridge club may decide to meet on the eve of the family reunion. My taxes may be used to support purposes which I as a churchperson profess to be immoral.

It is the purpose of this exercise to help you to focus in on yourself as a person living in society. It will certainly make you more conscious of what you decide and do as a participant not only in a religious community but in a variety of social groupings. It may help you to add new ethical dimensions to your thinking and decision making. Begin by looking upon yourself as a member of a religious society, a church or synagogue, or of whatever religious tradition you have. (If you do not have such explicit religious commitment or tradition, do the exercises in terms of your immersion into the "American way of life" and the values of civil religion which it enjoins, i.e., the things expected of a "good" American.)

This exercise is very simple. At the end of the week, reflect and note in your journal what things you have done during the week which responded to the explicit demands of the religious society or tradition of which you are a part. Page 51 may help you do this. Pick the one of these actions which seems most important or significant to you, one which you have stronger feelings attached to. Then use the following format to explore it further.

ACTION — What was it I did?

FEELINGS — What feelings accompanied my decision and my action? Would I have preferred to have not done it or put it off to another time? Was I eager to do it?

COST — What did it cost me to do this? Describe the material costs, costs of time, freedom, etc.

PAYOFF — What benefits actually accrue to me as a result of having performed this action? To others? What benefits do I expect?

PENALTIES — What actual penalties would I be liable to if I did not perform the action? What were my fears or catastrophic fantasies about what could possibly happen?

CONFLICTS — Did my action conflict with the demands of some other society to which I belong? What society? What demands?

ALTERNATIVES — What possible alternative courses of action were open to me? Ways of modifying my action?

If you are working with a group, there are two ways to proceed.

One approach: Participants may do the work in advance in their journals or on page 52, then share from it and discuss its feelings and implications in the group. In this case discussion replaces writing.

Some questions you might begin with are:

Which elements did you encounter which you have in common?
Which things were unique to individuals in your group?
Did you defy any of these norms?
What were the consequences or the feared consequences?

Since you've done the work privately in advance, you might share with each other what the experience of keeping this record was like for each of you. What parts of it were difficult? What rewarding? What disappointing?

Secondly, share whatever you feel comfortable with of your experience of sanctions, experiences of what happened to you when your values ran counter to those of your religious society or the people who were around you. What is your worst possible fantasy of what can happen to you if you behave differently? What did you learn about yourself in this inquiry? You may be helpful to each other in this process by asking for clarifications when needed to get an over-all picture of the social setting — what you understand to be taking place in the social interaction. Again, keep in mind our guidelines for discussions: avoid analyzing, avoid piggybacking on each other's feelings and experiences, and avoid leading questions. After you do this you might be conscious of how the group you are in right now affects your presentation — another example of the subtleties of our response to social situations.

A second approach: The work may actually be done when the group meets. Break the group into threesomes and have the participants of the subgroups take turns asking the above questions of each other about actions they each choose to talk about. Wrap up with a brief group discussion of the experience allowing each member to give his or her impressions to the reassembled large group.

Living in a Religious Society 51

The name or description of the religious society or tradition to which I belong.

_____

Things I have done this week which respond to the demands of this society or tradition.

ACTION:

FEELINGS:

COST:

PENALTIES:

CONFLICTS:

ALTERNATIVES:

A Continuing Process

You may wish to review your behavior in other than religious social groupings. What things did you do because they were a political or legal necessity, such things as paying your taxes, voting, being careful not to park in a No-Parking Zone, etc.? Look at each of the societies to which you belong, your family, your school, your community. Use the worksheet on page 54 to identify the ones most important to you. What are the concrete demands that each society makes on you? List them on the worksheet, making a special note of the things which you do which you would not have done at all or perhaps would have put off until another time, but which were demanded by these societies in which you participate. Use your journal to observe how you are affected by social sanctions.

> *What happens to you when your values run counter to the values of society or the group you happen to be in, or the individual persons you are with? In other words, in those kinds of situations what forces do you feel urging you to behave or speak one way or another?*
>
> *What sanctions do you feel threatened by from outside and from within yourself?*
>
> *How do you respond to these pressures?*
>
> *When you disagree with someone or have an opinion which not many other people around you hold and you are exchanging ideas with people on this subject, how do you behave?*
>
> *Do you rationalize your opinion to make it fit in? Do you dissimulate it in some fashion? Hide it? Do you resist? Do you keep quiet? Do you counterattack?*

Take a careful look at yourself in these coming days and write about your experiences in your journal. Record instances of such conflict of value or opinion and as you record them, of course, remember to make sure that you tell what happened as specifically and clearly as possible. Give sufficient detail to enable yourself to reconstruct the situation when you reread it. In other words, don't generalize, analyze and draw conclusions. For example, instead of writing, "I usually close up when I meet resistance to my ideas," write what actually took place; for example, "When Alice contradicted my opinion of the movie, *The Exorcist,* as we were sitting at supper with friends tonight I felt embarrassed. I sat back and withdrew from the conversation. Later on I very timidly told my closest friend John, who was sitting next to me, that Alice had misunderstood what I said and that actually my opinion was very similar to hers." Being specific aids self-discovery and growth.

54 JOURNAL FOR LIFE

IDENTIFYING ELEMENTS OF SOCIAL CONTROL

On each of the arrows numbered on to five, write the name of one of the five most important communities which you belong to — they may be state, family, school, work, club, etc. — whichever ones you feel most responsible to.

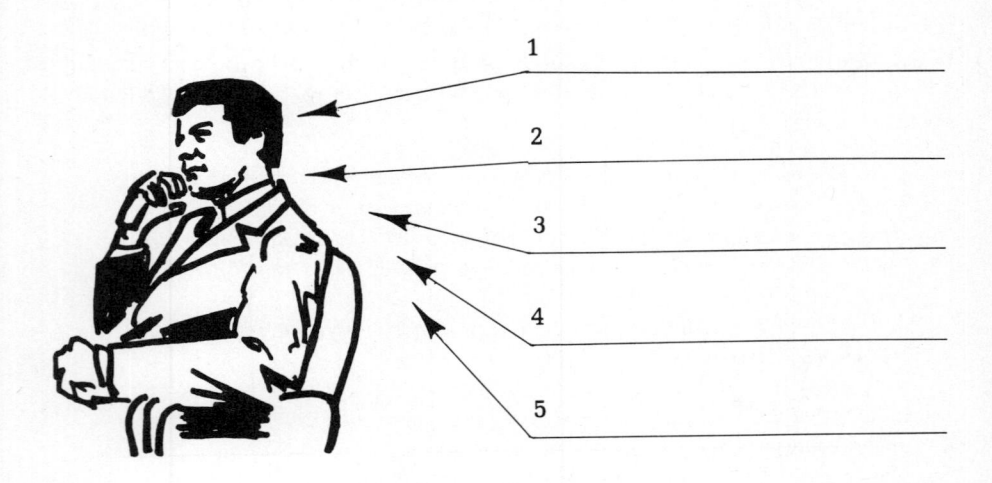

1.

2.

3.

4.

5.

Then in the boxes numbered one to five, list some of the explicit demands each of these makes on you, particularly those things which you have found yourself doing which you might not have wanted to do either at the time you did them or perhaps not at all. Use your journal as a resource for your observations.

1	2	3	4	5

Notes for the Group Leader

This exercise, depending on the nature of the group's involvement with it, may leave some individuals feeling quite powerless and depressed about their ability to control their own lives and actions or affect their religious institutions. If it seems that this is the direction of the discussion, the leader might insert these elements into the discussion:

Societies, their pressures and demands are a real and inevitable part of each person's existence. They serve needs as well as make demands.

We are looking at subtle social pressures not just to see how susceptible we are to them but that by becoming aware of them we may experience greater freedom, more alternatives in dealing with them.

The concluding chapter will provide some alternatives to the social pressures we feel.

8
Breakthroughs

The light died in the low clouds. Falling snow drank in the dusk. Shrouded in silence, the branches wrapped me in their peace. When the boundaries were erased, once again the wonder: That I exist.
Dag Hammarskjold

Surely the best alternative to "getting a fix" is not needing one, and this comes by taking care of ourselves, our values and our society all along. In a world where technology, not faith is moving mountains we tend to assume that the answer to every problem is to blast through with all our energies and our hardware. Rash, frustrating, and violent decisions and actions easily result. We attack when we could come to terms with the opponent. We drive ourselves to nervous breakdowns with endless hours of intensity. We disemploy people with machines. We choose sterilization for societies which multiply too fast. The pat answer to technology's present ills is inevitably more technology.

But we do have other resources beyond our mechanical and chemical inventiveness as useful, impressive and necessary as these may at times be. They are, in fact, resources which, whether we are conscious of them as such or not, are at the root of our ability to function in a human way even at the technological level. I call the exercise of these resources "breakthroughs" because they are ways of breaking through impasses, ways of our escaping the feeling of being trapped, means of replenishing exhausted resources, vantage points for new perspectives. Some of them are things which we have or may choose to have in common; others may be unique to individuals among us, developed out of our singular personal experience.

Looking for Breakthroughs

We will conclude this excursion into theology from experience by an inventory of our own breakthroughs, the spiritual resources available to us as we go forth to meet the day. Here is a list of some of the common ones and some questions with each, which you might answer in your journal or discuss in your group to explore the part that they play in your life:

> PLAY — When I can abandon myself to fantasy and play, the everyday world can be seen in a different perspective. What part does play have in my life? What are favorite forms of play? Humor? Dance? Physical exercise and body movement? Games? Diversions? Hobbies?
>
> HOPES — Hope is an opening out to a different future. It also relativizes the present, sees it as changeable. What are some of my hopes? Complete the sentence, "I hope . . ." in a half dozen different ways. Which hopes do I let grow in me? Which ones do I dismiss?
>
> PRAYER — A conversation with God, a free flow of feeling in faith. The place where I can expose and explore my deepest needs and desires without social sanctions and inner censoring.

What is prayer like for me? When, how do I pray? What important resolutions and solutions have come through prayer? Worship?

MYSTICAL MOMENTS — Times in which I felt lost in another person, place, thing or event. Moments of unity, joy, timelessness, ecstasy. What things in my life are most conducive to this oneness, a child, a flower, a snowfall, a verse of scripture? Find some of these things.

DISCOVERY — Remember the experience of struggling with a difficult problem and how I felt when the solution welled up within. What discoveries have I made? What are some of the breakthrough moments in my personal story? When and where have important discoveries taken place for me?

OUTRAGE — The energy that comes when my sense of justice or love is violated in events and encounters. When have I sensed outrage? What was the result? What things do I want to rearrange in my life, my environment?

OTHER BREAKTHROUGHS — What other experiences have been breakthroughs for me? Vacations? Conversations? Rest? Illnesses? Think of some of the major impasses of your life? How did resolution come?

Before You Begin — A Perspective

To borrow a theological perspective, breakthroughs are always *grace*. That is, they cannot be earned or bought, achieved or merited. They always come as *gifts*. Even this may be hard to understand, because true gifts are rarities in our world. Instead of spontaneous bounty, which like creation is a lifegiving act, we have gift exchanges, expense account bribes and advertisers' holidays for mother, father and the dog. The gift that is expected, owed, earned or paid back is not a gift at all. It is a business transaction or worse. It neither creates nor redeems. It corrupts and imprisons. It is deadly. All that we are capable of with respect to true gifts, besides giving them, is asking for them and receiving them gratefully when they come our way.

Let me illustrate this a bit further from my own experience, my own theology. Many years ago I used to take part in a radio dialogue (argument) on a call-in night show. It was the classical setup, priest vs. atheistic humanist. One of the arguments which Rick, my affectionate disbelieving colleague would bring forth as we sought to rescue each other and radio listeners everywhere from ignorance and error, ran thus: "If God is moved by prayer, God is not God. For God, to be perfect, i.e., to be God, God must be immovable and unchangeable, incapable of being swayed in any direction. Either then, there is no God, or, the gods that Christians, Jews and other believers pray to so foolishly are not true gods at all." I used to counter the argument by emphasizing the "eternal perspective" which gave God foreknowledge of all that would be asked — therefore God always knew and did not need to be moved by our petitions to grant them. God let us ask because that was the human way; it was a condescension to our nature. Perhaps. Yet it appears to me that there is a far better solution to the apparent contradiction posed by my friend. It seems obvious now as I observe more mature giving on the part of individuals in my life. God both listens and gives in perfect freedom. No amount of my wheedling overpowers God's will, nor does God give with strings attached. Thus, what God gives is truly gift, grace, and to be received well must be experienced as such. God's is the listening and giving of a fully actualized personality, a way of perceiving and acting which seems like a contradiction only because we are so little capable of it, not because it is inherently impossible. This theology has been the result of my experiences of giving and getting.

One does not, I think, have to be a believer to share the meaning of this. Whether I speak in traditional religious terms of "sin and grace," "flesh and spirit," "idolatry and fear of the Lord," or simply of slavery and freedom or of dehumanization and liberation, we can share a theology of experience. For if these things have meaning they must, among other things refer to the encroachment of the mechanistic and scientific and of the political and economic systems on our nature and of the power of breakthrough experiences to shatter their hold on us and restore more abundant life to us.

Breakthroughs are not things we cause to happen, but events which we *allow* to happen. Our role is definitely that of receivers, but this does not imply that we must always be perfectly passive at all times — the moment of breakthrough will itself take care of that for us. We can hope or pray for breakthroughs, remove obstacles, turn in new directions, then step back and look, relax our grip and let things happen. We can become more receptive by an increased awareness of the breakthroughs in our life story, as we are attempting here. This may not directly cause us to have more of them, but, by pointing in the directions whence they come can show us some ways of becoming more receptive and less resistant. It is possible for us to discover something of the lifestyle and the activities which make them more likely to occur for us. This in turn may provide some of the direction we want our lives to follow.

Making the Inventory

Begin your inventory now.
Start by using just one of the categories provided above or with one significant breakthrough experience of your own personal story. Describe it in some detail.

How does it feel to you now? What learnings does it contain? Make sure you are satisfied with this exploration before moving on to other breakthroughs.

When you have done several, perhaps you will see emerging something of the lifestyle and attitudes which make breakthroughs possible and most probable for you.

In Your Group

If you do this work together with others, each person might select just one breakthrough activity or event to write about. Use your journal or the worksheet on page 61. Take twenty minutes or so to do this. Then allow each person to share what he or she wishes to of the writing or the experience of writing about breakthroughs. If your group is large, you might like to divide into pairs or threesomes to do the initial sharing and then report back to the whole group later about your discussion. Some things you might discuss as a whole group are:

What breakthrough experiences seem most common in your group?

Which experiences are unique?

Are there breakthrough activities reported by some members that others would like to experience?

Have there been any breakthrough experiences in your life as a group? What were they? How did they feel to those who experienced them?

Since this is the last programmed session with these Theology from Experience *materials, are there things which you would like to say to each other, to specific members of the group, which you will feel unhappy about if you leave them unsaid?*

Notes for Group Leaders

This is the last session in this series. You may plan to meet again, reusing some of the approaches provided in the various exercises in this program. If you do, it may be important to negotiate with the group for a certain number of meetings to follow so that their commitment to each other has a specific end in view. If this is your last meeting, be sure to save some time at its close for any unfinished business which participants may feel with the process or unsaid things they would like to express to each other.

A BREAKTHROUGH INVENTORY

Appendix

Some Guidelines for Discussing These Exercises With Others.

Five initial guidelines are discussed in the Appendix to the *Foundations* volume of *Journal for Life:*

1. *Don't Misuse Pronouns.*
2. *Don't Argue About Somebody Else's Feelings or Experiences.*
3. *Avoid Leading Questions.*
4. *Avoid Analyzing.*
5. *Be As Specific, Immediate and Concrete as Possible.*

To these, we now add the following:

6. *Talk to Others, Not About Them.*

   Conversation in a group maintains a higher level of energy when we speak specifically to each other. So, for example, if I have been impressed by something said by another member of my group, instead of saying (vaguely, to the group in general) "Joe's story of his experience with the death of his wife was very moving," I might more effectively look at Joe and speak directly to him, "Joe, I was very moved by the story you told of your wife's death. Thank you for sharing it with me." It helps to look directly at others and speak *to* them even when asking questions, and to use their names when addressing them. It will usually be more satisfying to ask specifically one or two or more members of my group, whose opinion would be more important to me, to answer a question than to just let it sail out undirected in the group. If I ask one or several persons in succession for their opinion, I will have the satisfaction of getting answers from the people whose answers I want, and the group will know that the question and the need behind it has been dealt with. The group members will not be left hanging, wondering whether they have responded sufficiently to me, whether I am finished or still unsatisfied. In time you will find that making better contact with others in this way not only improves the level of interaction in your group. It will help you to know better what it is you wish to communicate and aid you in expressing it more clearly. Experimenting with this form of direct address in journal writing which concerns others in your experience will be helpful in resolving your inner conflicts with them.

7. Take Care of Yourself.

It is up to you, not to the leader or the other members of the group, to make sure that you say what you want to say when you want to say it. Some persons in groups habitually feel guilty about using the group's time for their own needs, fearing that they are monopolizing time that does not belong to them. Your ideas and feelings are what makes a group exchange worthwhile. Others are looking for them from you. Holding back may well deprive everyone of a good experience. If, on occasion a group member actually does monopolize the discussion, this too should be dealt with openly and directly.

8. Don't Invalidate Others' Experiences.

This is an extension of the second guideline. We invalidate others' experiences by: A) trivialization, e.g., "That's unimportant." "That doesn't really count."; B) by attacking the mode in which the experience exists, e.g., "It's in your head." "That's just a product of your imagination."; C) by attacking the content of the experience, e.g., "It never happened that way at all."; D) By attacking the person's capacity or right to have the experience, e.g., "You should be ashamed to tell such a story." "That's offensive."*
These forms of invalidation are experienced by almost everyone in our society. After a while, we interiorize them. Thus, it may be valuable for you to observe whether you censor yourself in these ways when speaking to others or writing in your journal.

9. Press For Language That Makes Good Contact.

When speaking or listening, we need to make good contact with each other if real communication is to take place. Some patterns of speech behavior are obstacles to this. Learn to recognize and avoid them. Here are some examples: A) jargon, like most mass produced things, becomes trite, canned and empty. When jargon appears, encourage the speaker to take an individual, personal and creative approach to re-expressing what he or she really wants to say. B) *Yes-but* and *If only* are two common ways of softening the real message.

---

* cf. R. D. Laing, *Politics of Experience,* (New York: Ballantine, 1967), p. 36.

Yes, I'd love to come to your dinner, *but* I'm not sure I'm free that evening. *If only* you had time to practice, you would be a better tennis player. In these kinds of statements, it may not be at all clear where the emphasis is, what the speaker's actual message is meant to be. C) Talking too much: The person who monopolizes the conversation, over-explains or repeats everything until it is dead, incontestable, unquestionable and complete (and usually boring), is taking the heat off him/herself by preventing real contact and exchange. Note, I am talking here not about the person who talks frequently or at length but of the person whose tactic is a hit and run kind of verbosity, the individual who puts things out in such a way that engagement with the speaker is impossible.*

10. Handle With Care.

No facet of small group work has caused more anxiety for the general public than that of physical contact. "Touchy-feely" became the derogatory adjective for encounter groups, whether they deserved it or not. Stories of "goings-on" both true and false contributed to wariness of artificiality and insincerity in group processes. All forms of human communication, certainly speech far more than gesture or contact, need to be tested for authenticity. On the other hand, I do not think that it can be denied that the culture that many of us were reared in as well as the attitudes which prevail in large parts of our present society have surrounded touching with strong taboos, often incapacitating us and depriving us of a whole world of human expression. Taboos tend to make forbidden things both dangerous and exciting. Thus it is hard to overcome them without uneasiness and discomfort. Restoring the natural fluidity of our emotional outreach to each other is a struggle often resisted initially, explored with anxiety and achieved with awkwardness. What first emerges in a group of people who begin to make this breakthrough seems to be "phony," and is immediately dubbed so. (People are not so quick to note the ongoing phoniness of repeatedly aborting our inner feelings and impulses in the name of the ideal of preserving a calm, impassive, "cool" exterior.) It is important, then, for the members of a group to recognize these initial tottering steps for what they are, the beginnings of new learning. These first awkward attempts to increase the range of our emotional and tactile expressions of caring may be awkward, but they are not artificial. The fact that we must discuss the subject causes perhaps more problems than it resolves. Our guideline is simple, *Handle with Care,* touch with caring. I believe that this best part of ourselves behaves this way. It is a question of letting it emerge

---

* cf. E. & M. Polster, *Gestalt Therapy Integrated,* (New York: Brunner-Mazel, 1973), pp. 156-157.

out from under the baggage of culture and the "no-nos" of personal history which tend to bury it in us. Let me close by sharing with you the most sensitive words which I have heard about this topic:

> *It is the same with regard to the physical expression of group love. Some find it easy to embrace. Some find it difficult. Undoubtedly it is our experience that the physical expression of love within a group, by touching, by embracing, by sharing . . . promotes peace and trust, diminishes the sexual tensions that rise from loneliness, and can on occasion heal the mentally disturbed. Yet here too, detachment has to be learned. One has to be clear about one's own motivation. Rather solemnly, some echo of St. Paul comes to mind, telling me that the freedom of the Spirit should not be made the cloak of license. It is a delicate area to walk in. One's own need for love should never have first place. Otherwise there is a constant danger that Eros the horse will buck off the rider Agape. Here too each member of a community must be free to move gently and learn by mistakes.* *

11. Do Not Make Absolutes Out Of Personal Experiences.

Because I have had an experience or feel a certain way about someone or something does not at all mean that others have had the same experiences or feel the same way. Particularly in discussions with others it is important not to make the assumptions that others are having the same thoughts or sensing the same things as I. If I suspect perceptions or feelings similar to my own exist in others, it is important to "check it out" by asking how others see something or react to it, before proceeding as if everybody agreed with my assessment. Certainly our experiences tell us about the nature of things and people. Most of the time however, they are only fragmentary glances. We can learn from each other by putting these fragmentary glances together. Sharing feelings can be a strong antidote to prejudice and fear. This is not to deny that my experiences are learnings for me — rather it is to assert that they are, but to admit that the truth they contain may be partial and peculiar to me. For example, to assert "Little brothers are pests" is an unfounded absolute projection of the truth of my experience which is "I feel pestered by Jamie, who makes a habit of interrupting me when I'm talking to my fiance on the telephone." Usually statements like this don't cause great harm, and certainly you will find others to

---

* Baxter, James K., *Jerusalem Daybook,* (Wellington, New Zealand: Price-Milburn, 1968), pp. 1-2.

agree that little brothers can have pesky qualities. The point is, not a great lot is communicated either. But there are times when it can be damaging or even disastrous to project the meaning of an experience into an absolute, making a judgment about the value of an experience in terms which suggest that it is bad or good or true or false for others or for all people or even for myself in all times and situations. Assumptions like "All men are —." or "All women are —." can keep us from meeting each other. They can be the stereotypes which destroy marriages and friendships before they are made.

Approaches to Journal Keeping:

Hughes, Milt, *SPIRITUAL JOURNEY NOTEBOOK,* National Student Ministries, 127 Ninth Ave., North, Nashville, Tennessee 37234: 1974, $5.50 "A Guide for personal spiritual growth through developing basic disciplines and specific actions in the Christian life."

Progoff, Ira, *AT A JOURNAL WORKSHOP,* Dialogue House Library, 45 West 10th Street, New York 10011: 1975, $12.50 "The basic text and guide for using the Intensive Journal."

Simons, George F., *JOURNAL FOR LIFE:* Part 1, Life in Christ, Division of ACTA, Foundation for Adult Catechetical Teaching Aids. Order from: Publishers Services, 155 E. Ohio Street, Chicago 60611. 1975, $1.45 "Discovering faith and values through journal keeping."